In a Strange Land

In a Strange Land

Introducing Ten Kingdom Poets

EDITED BY

D. S. MARTIN

CASCADE *Books* • Eugene, Oregon

IN A STRANGE LAND
Introducing Ten Kingdom Poets

Poiema Poetry Series 33

Cascade Books
An Imprint of Wipf and Stock Publishers
199 W. 8th Ave., Suite 3
Eugene, OR 97401

www.wipfandstock.com

PAPERBACK ISBN: 978-1-5326-7773-1
HARDCOVER ISBN: 978-1-5326-7774-8
EBOOK ISBN: 978-1-5326-7775-5

Cataloguing-in-Publication data:

Names: Martin, D. S., editor.

Title: In a strange land : introducing ten kingdom poets / edited by D. S. Martin.

Description: Eugene, OR: Cascade Books, 2019 | Series: Poiema Poetry Series 31

Identifiers: ISBN 978-1-5326-7773-1 (paperback) | ISBN 978-1-5326-7774-8 (hardcover) | ISBN 978-1-5326-7775-5 (ebook)

Subjects: LCSH: Poetry—21st century

Classification: PS3626 G3707 T87 2019 (paperback) | PS3626 (ebook).

Manufactured in the U.S.A.   09/16/19

In memory of
Anya Krugovoy Silver
(1968—2018)

CONTENTS

Susan Cowger

PREFACE

Ever since we were expelled from the Garden, ever since the banishing of Cain, we have found ourselves time and again living in a strange land. Often it is as a foreigner like Abraham having obediently wandered far from home, sometimes like Moses who has fled for his life, or like the Israelites by the rivers of Babylon who have been taken into captivity and wonder, *How shall we sing the Lord's song in a strange land?* (Psalm 137).

Sometimes we find that the land of our raising has grown strange to us—as livelihoods disappear, family members move further away, cities rapidly grow, and values change. Sometimes we find ourselves in the valley of the shadow of death, forsaken by a friend, or in the grip of depression. Often when we read where another human speaks truthfully about living in a strange land—even if it is not exactly what we are going through—we feel less alone.

This poetry collection gathers into one volume works by ten talented poets who eloquently express their experiences. They are each well deserving of having their own full-length poetry books, but (at least at the time of this writing) have not quite reached that milestone. Each poet has a different story. Some have published extensively, some have published chapbooks, some come from other artistic disciplines—music or visual arts—and some have been quietly and beautifully doing their thing without the ambition of making a big deal out of what they've been doing. But others have noticed, and so this book seeks to draw your attention to them.

The Poiema Poetry Series is all about providing a home for the finest poetry by people of Christian faith. *In A Strange Land: Introducing Ten Kingdom Poets* further follows that same path.

Soli Deo Gloria,

D. S. Martin
Orvieto, Italy
April, 2019

DEBBIE SAWCZAK

Georgetown, Ontario

Unseen and Hoped For

And the Kingdom of heaven is also like
the fetus in the ultrasound photo:
the one you can only see if you already love,
and seeing, love still more.

Someone who knows shows you the heart—
so small!—
beating in the noise of curved lines,
and thenceforth you never forget where it is,
cherish that luminous spot until
one far day you are given the child
and can look straight into its eyes.

Snow Falling on the City

The way things look through falling snow:
all the more lovely for lack of resolution;
a pointillist painting,
all the hues less saturated,
like echoes,
reminiscences.

1

Then and Now

I lived so loved by you,
then,
was so welcome inside your life;
found strange how strong and thrilling
it spilled out in poems,
how huge it caused my heart to become,
and how trusting my tongue:
I said more for your ears than I thought I had voice for,
I, shy,
faster to flee than a fawn;
this time I stayed.

Now you seem almost gone,
one hand on the doorknob,
your keys in the other,
their jingle giving the lie to your patient words;
my cheekbones tingle beneath the tears forming,
as you linger politely, uttering nothings.
I bite my lip.

But I'm not going to ask why this is, now,
for you never answer such questions.
And I'm not going to run now, either:
this is one undertaking I will not quit.
Besides, it's already too late:
my heart has been permanently stretched to include your large,
    sharp, and angular shape
and will never shrink back.

One Colour Missing

I'm almost used to this almost-peace.
Then memories sharp with points, like stars,
emerge
and clutter the sky;
like a tight-coiled spring
or a jack-in-the box one jars by accident,
ache comes unsquashed,
and flies in my unwary eye.

It's as if the world had one colour missing,
were a poem composed without the letter 'e',
or a wobbly table that nothing fits under the leg of.

I have gamely tried every road,
wish I could get to wherever you've gone;
if you'd shout from there,
I would leap to my feet,
tuck my head,
and sprint toward the sound.

Contingent Order

Gravity works,
electrons work,
sound works—those three little bones;
the water cycle works,
ligaments work,
light works on rods and cones,
and images backwards and upside down on our retinas
come out right.
Alleluia!

Baby

after Hopkins

Sweet sigh-scent of slight hair,
light body built fine,
fluff-lined flannel, layered over tight-fold fingers:
all quiet.

Then loud blue yells,
red face taut round the tiny-tongue quiver,
eyes shut squeeze tears;
wee small lungs heave hard for one long still second,
gather, pump more cries;
searing sad sound breaks all hearing hearts,
mostly mother's: mere she
can't cure every deep-drowned dark.

But often after dry clothes, milk drunk, sleep:
wonder-shine eyes wake wide, look round,
find yours;
hands up: *handle me!*
Laugh, soft-lift little bundle,
press close-firm,
compact:
calm-peace.

Breathe warm, rock, stroke silk-smooth neck—
and rejoice: one wobbly-head daredevil dares trust you,
rests whole holy trust
in the you God gave.

Wind on the Trail

Pausing our linear progress on the Bruce,
on the boardwalk by the pond
we watch laced trees of all species
in a tall wall ringing the water:
a brisk stiff breeze is riffling the leaves
and rafting the boughs on its undulous swell,
so fluidly,
gracefully—
not like a gale's wild lashing; yet
somehow animated as one,
they dance so strong in different directions.

The other day a guy said
whoever did not tick the doctrinal boxes
he ID'd
must not be moved by the Spirit.

I disagreed.

I Never Saw This Before

So this is what it's like when your dad is dying.
His faraway voice puts a periscope into my hand
and I peer up over grey walls
at hills of green.
His eyes are my porthole—
in the belly of my own slow ship I gaze out,
glimpse land on the horizon
between the waves that wipe out my view.
He smiles at unknowable distant things
and a window opens in my basement;
a breeze enters, shifts old papers on my desk.

To Mary (Mark 3:21)

When you came to fetch him home
'cause you thought he was crazy,
did you not recall
pondering all those things in your heart:
the sight of Gabriel aglow in your bedroom,
the hymn flowing out of you swift like a river,
the leap of Elizabeth's child in her belly;

that story of airy choirs at midnight
over the fields beyond Bethlehem,
the shepherds' knuckles white on their staffs
as they entered the stable,
and then when they saw him,
how alarm drained from their frames
as they sank on the straw at the manger's edge;

those courtly foreigners
who'd spent quiet decades
uncovering hidden meanings
laying their treasures down for his kingship
and touching the ground with their foreheads;

how when you lost him on the long way home
he turned up cool in the Temple,
unrepentant,
talking at twelve with ancients listening intently?

Did you not think of all this then,
when it seemed he was out of his mind
defying demons?

Story of the One Man (Ephesians 2:11–19)

When I was a boy of thirteen
they milled about the gate
on the wall's other side,
their eyes cast down
by our sidewise gaze
as we set out for home after worship,
Abba and me.

One boy my age dared look me in the eye.
His father had the lightened face of forgiven penitence,
and his murmured prayer in uncouth Latin syllables
of caesars and soldiers
had the earnest ring of reality
I sometimes heard in my father's.
But I knew those lawless and uncircumcised,
their longing notwithstanding,
had God's love less.
You've no business here,
I felt like saying;
your unclean idol prayers will not be heard.
But I only scowled and spit.
He scuffed dung-flecked dust in our general direction
with the toe of his sandal.

No way that wall could fall,
Abba had said,
let alone be rebuilt in three days.

But at thirty, at night on my bed,
I knew.
Not all the blood of bulls and turtledoves,
tithes,
recited psalms
or prayers
would erase that writ.

That all seems like another, long-ago life.
We worship now in a Temple not made by hands
—One without a wall.
Gaius and I are forty.
In pale dawn
on the Day of Remembering the Rising,
we sit down side by side,
sip wine,
hand round hunks of holy bread
and sing.

John 13:1

And having loved those who were his in the world
he loved them to the end.

Here's how you love us, then:
before the world's foundation,
and while knitting us in the womb;
wooing us from our first day's light,
through years of fumbling, falling, dancing,
weeping, doubting, laughing—
the whole bewildering way into our graves;
you love us deep and deeper, down
to your own vicarious grave,
and clear on out to the Rising,
our foe your footstool.

You love us full to Kingdom come,
till the cows come home,
to the end:
us, who are yours in the world.

LAURA REECE HOGAN

Los Angeles, California

Nocturne

Silk of a thousand shades flows from your throat, night
notes billow, float, dance in the sleeping garden, tangle
of rosebush the shadowed lectern of your liturgy. Star
beams cannot find your gray body but fiery sparks issue

from open beak: scrub jay shriek melts into lilt of robin,
goldfinch warble sharpens to hawk cry, hoot owl, medley
of sky and tree. You wing wide, embrace all nations of the
tongue, a writer of icons, singing doorways of egg and gold

and open eyes, a call to the soaring beyond. You chant the
quilt of creation, hymn to fingers that wove the fabric of
melody, conducted patterns of feather, flight and fugue.
Now the phoebe's sweet chirp, swallow's chatter, scraping

crow-caw, you swallow the wide world whole just to croon
your divine office, embroider blessing on the hours, lauds
in blackness. Mockingbird, you settle on my chimney top
like a church steeple, trilling frogsong, the cricket's hum,

burbling laugh of the neighbor child. You chat, you rasp,
chirrup, scold. You sing sunlight in the darkness, telling
cocoons and keening coyotes how we were knitted to love,
endure, and even in the cleft of night, joy in spilling praise.

Good Fruit

Children of Eve, are we free now? Or does the fruit,
once consumed, consume us still? All these mornings after

gnawing at the core, are *we* gnawed at the core, known
for our knowing, lost to a wholeness lying somewhere west

of our hunger, somewhere long excised in our memory,
but desired in our flesh, our cells homing to an Eden

like serpent-stung pushovers pining in a strange land?
By all rights the tree should bear no apricots, decayed

half-corpse, all broken sagging arms and knobby elbows,
the brittleness longing for the sap of youth, her maidenhood

quickened at the dawn of the world, up from a rib her roots.
She grew strong, smooth; her fruit burst golden sweetness.

A shimmering spider strand crosses her wrecked branches,
catches silver in the morning sun, arrows bright toward

impossible leaves greening, orbs of yellow ripening. Her side
splits with spark irrepressible, mother of the living again.

Her divided body forms one being. Children of Eve, despite
our fruit, do we all house deadness? Or despite all failure,

might we glint good light, push on to green, to gold?

Cherith

Before you sent me down to the wadi there was
that goldfinch, shining.
swaying, it lingered   warbled, flew away,
away   away to the blue mountain, each beat of wing
a stop in my heart—stay
stay, stay   the shadow of your bird
in me shifted, my love slipped the green and lilac
banks of the river, beyond rushes and the reaches
of my throat.

Then those days wheeled on the track, puffing,
mechanical and drawn. A thousand tongues choked
on salt, not bread. I turned, turned into a pillar looking
for your warm yellow breast.

A drought later I forgot to remember, how you had taken
yourself away from me   my reshaped heart steadied,
bundles and branches worn into grooves, patience
uncounted.

Is that why you sent me down to Cherith, to hide me
in your hands, to drink of the stream in cool deep swallows?
sometimes I am afraid to touch the beauty of the emerald
mossy stones, they make me ache with riparian joy

Your goldfinches alight, feed me presence and song, and it is for
this your finest wheat   I have longed.

There is One Splendor of the Sun

1 Cor. 15:41, 2 Cor. 4:10

the moon holds another brightness, a bare seed caressed by
fire-clothed luminosity,
      lighting the glass darkly, a half-veiled face,

like half the body of fire-scorched acacia, Icarus-cracked
crepe leaves of lunar glint,
      half the body alight in sun, a shining green

humility, budding fresh, an untouched life. We too always
carry about such celestial
      half-lidded brilliance, a body chiaroscuro,

the dying of Jesus, so that our uncrucified lives show out,
leafy laughing crown still
      anchored branch, trunk, root, deep in soil,

a blackness musky with moondark, loam of the longing night.
One needs the other.
      His star fell down and dimmed for us,

to spark our candles awake, to flame alive molecules, shoots
from the shimmering vine.
      An eclipse serves well to darken us,

a reflecting body only, moon carrying about in it the lantern,
lightning in a bottle,
      splendor borrowed   yet burning in the body of the living.

Organic Ink

Petals unfold from your tongue, you speak crimson
velvet freshness into being. An opening bud of careful
precision, a floral life floating on your breath, bees, and boundary.

You expand a mystery of molecules, at your word atomic spice
springs into breeze; you dizzy hummingbirds, intoxicate butterflies.
Shining beams play, shimmer, light your Shulamite, invite a tango.

You draw. Come, find my notes poured out in the garden, etched among
lemons and limes. See, the lost apricot awakens! Sweet shoots adorn
black crumbling branches. On every cell I inscribe: what was dead is alive.

You wait for me to discover your love among the leaves and thorns,
(will I perceive it?) your hidden blossom of wonder, a shy heart-shaped
valentine of third heaven, a sachet for this moment, a marked downbeat

of song, a bodily inhale of my eyes and skin and hair and breath. Filled
with rising melody, your unspoken lyrics whispered on wind, I join
your written roses in swaying dance, in blood-red bloom of belonging.

Litany of Flights

First, the winged movement, steady, forward. Scrub jays in flitting
progress, hawks in predator glide, a ringing up, a knife-sharp slope

down. Second, the effortless type, wind-splayed, motionless pinions
in thermal recline, as the Psalmist says, blessings breeze his love even

in sleep. Third, the hungry, against the gale, the destination singular
and the sun dipping crimson. Fourth, the metallic, business or pleasure.

Fifth, the whirring kind, all hummingbird. A picnic, apples and chocolate
in the garden with roses, both flower and child. You miss it when it's gone.

Sixth, a baffling flight of stairs, winding upward, passage and yet vehicle,
spiraling to unseen landings—hope courses in the kaleidoscopic lights.

Seventh, soar to the sun. Eighth, melt in bitter hubris. You know the story.
Ninth, escape. A flight out of Egypt, a path through the sea cleared by

divine hand. The times you ran, the times you were left behind in lament.
Tenth, only rotting in the belly of a whale tames your stubborn turn from

Nineveh. Eleventh, flights of despair and of yearning, two sides of one
letting go, hard-earned release back into the wild, unbound by expectation,

featherlike. Twelfth, in a moment, caught up high by the Beloved, the one
making all things work together, wings, body, arch, air—caught up, like the

Shulamite bride, to regions beyond aeronautical wisdom, transported in joy.
See, he says, the painful paring of your hollow bones has made you light.

The Eyes I Have Desired

"O spring like crystal!/ If only, on your silvered-over faces,/ you would suddenly form/ the eyes I have desired,/ which I bear sketched deep within my heart." John of the Cross, "The Spiritual Canticle"

Like a bride I walk upon petals,
cobalt florets kiss my arms as they

tumble, soft stars beneath my feet.
Panicles of lavender dot perfect above

in jacaranda and sky, Ezekiel's
sapphire throne of God glints,

cirrus angels touch leaden angles of
horizon. Scrub jays call, arrow azure.

All this falling down from heaven, so
fleeting, yet my momentary eyes

meet firmament, the unmoved
moving intensity of blue gaze.

For one long caught breath, even the hawks
swing down for me.

Revelation

Last night did you see the lightning,
like silvered bolts in a basin of
purple cloud? No thunder at all,

she says, only shards of light.
I made her drive me up to the top
of the mountain, just to watch.

Here she turns to her sister,
smile answering smile.
God is in everything,

everywhere I look; this morning
in a swallowtail out of nowhere.
Her quiet words flutter and fold.

I am fluent in her tongue,
the faith-embered flash in her eyes.
Those bowls filled with electricity

in turn become my divine lightning;
there also alights his sudden butterfly:
in the easy love between two sisters

his wings open bright.

RYAN APPLE

Lansing, Michigan

The Atomic Weight of Glory

Before thumbing through that office magazine,
waiting to have a tooth filled,
you had never imagined yourself to be
such a walking chemistry kit.

Who knew manganese's tiny vial
held a skeleton key to your sundry moods?
Or that smuggled within your bloodstream
was a penny's worth of liquid gold?

So here you are: 34 pounds carbon,
4 pounds nitrogen,
then topped off with traces of tungsten,
caesium, chromium, arsenic—

till finally: *Just add water*.
And there accounts well more
than 99.9%—
plenty good enough. At least for some,

                        though not for you

ever since that breakfast on the canyon floor.
You hadn't even known you were hungry
till lightning flashed in a clear blue sky
revealing the frost to be wafers of bread.

And then, rushing down the cold ravine,
a strange wind filled your lungs,
tungsten formed a filament,
and your whole being shot

with light. You felt magnesium and phosphorus ignite
and burn within your bones,
fueled by a secret element
unperceived in the whole of the world.

Lighter than lithium,
more precious than gold,
and assurance of when—
yes, one fine day—

at last you will finally be whole.

Sonnet

O Christ, when you return to bring your reign
Will sleeping infants hear your trumpet call?
Are they invited to your banquet hall
Which welcomes in the poor, the blind, and lame?

Think of non-sentient stars, summoned by name—
These ancient lights like common sparrows fall.
You track our graying hairs; you count them all
And weigh an hour and century the same.

If you recall the smallest vein you knit
And stitch the robes the least of these will wear;
If you do not call nascent lungs unfit
But find within the faintest cries a prayer,
Then wake our daughter; dry a mother's tears,
And hundredfold redeem the stolen years.

Esau Returns From Meeting Jacob

I value his gifts less than bean soup and bread;
I don't need more sheep, and his motive's unclear—
each treacherous step of the way, he's misled.

My appetite's large, but it's sated, well fed
from hunting wild game, wilder women, strong beer;
his tokens are worth less than bean soup and bread.

I had sworn to kill him—he should be long dead,
but rage cooled to pity with each passing year,
and now I see clearly he too was misled:

this second-born son, prophesied to be head,
came haggard and limping, then bowing in fear,
and better off back with his bean soup and bread.

Like Abram and Isaac, he's certain God said
that Canaan will be his. I won't interfere
with Jacob's beliefs, even though he's misled.

Since God has a dreamland to give him, instead
I'll climb my own heaven, the rocky Mount Seir.
I value his gifts less than bean soup and bread.
                    (Each treacherous step of the way, he's misled.)

Sundown

Ephesians 4:26

In pre-marriage counseling they told us to never
let the sun go down on our anger.
Whimsy notwithstanding,

the warning seemed quaint
since electricity has deemed our clocks
the arbiters of time,

and sailors now watch weather.com,
having jettisoned their nursery rhymes
about red skies.

But in the wake of our disagreement,
with the sky so overcast
(I circled the same point;

turning, you drifted off),
I just stared into the clouded night, wondering
how we might navigate to common ground.

Opportunity

One time he took the devil's hand,
weary and famished, needing help
to finish the final ascent—

                              but oh what a view.

The Mediterranean blue,
ships of Sidon, Lebanon cedars
sparrows and screech owls
hillsides with thousands of sheep

Galileans casting nets
women at the well
blind men begging poolside
Herod's temple
the temple of Artemis

Pharaoh's magicians
Celtic druids
Brahmans and Sudra
pigs and pygmies
roving wolves, hungry lions
fattened calves, skittish sheep
                    how many million sheep?
sheep without a shepherd

The long way back was less picturesque.
Lonely rocks like loaves of bread
Mirages masking burning sand
(what of the promised desert streams?)

Illusions of Nazareth
Jerusalem
and then even Rome, how it could have
right then all been his

And who among his hearers would know
it was no hyperbole whenever he posed:
                    what good is the world in hand when
the seller demands your soul?

The Two-Edged Sword

How many times had I waved it around,
strolling through the camp, so cavalier,
humming *Onward Christian Soldiers*
or some other song of wars
which I knew nothing of?

How could I have known the pain
of its surgical strike through flesh
till my friend found me back in the tent
where he sliced me good and clean,
rending my marrow from bone?

As his arm swung back, I knew it was true
wounds from a friend can be trusted,
when the sword and swordsman are one
and the flashing steel illumines the scar
where the blade had pierced his heart.

Portrait of a Friend's Daughter, Senior Year

A warm September night, she tests her legs
on the trampoline. The air is humid, the grass
deep green and damp. Her springing

tells the tempo and time to all the songs of night:
the chorus of distant traffic, the buzz of insects
burrowed in trees, and the trill of the mockingbird stretching

its adolescent wings. But lately, she's been soaking in
the music of the spheres, the silence

planets and stars have sung from time only God can tell—
the profound and secret harmony she hears
alone. Her sister is already sleeping, her mother
busy in the kitchen. As for her father and me in the sunroom,

we have grown deaf to their song. The whole wide universe
is waking now around her, the starlight calling her higher;
bound by bound, she is breaking the spell of gravity.

Menarche

We dads see our daughters up to the gate
but do not enter that garden,
nor try to decipher those handwritten maps
they carefully carry inside.

Nature silently signals who should
and who should not enter her temple.

Cherry boughs shelter the sinuous path,
serpentine tendrils charm the wind,
and somewhere, the trees of knowledge and life
may be proven one and the same.

No angel guards the wrought iron fence;
only wildflowers fringing the border.

So few of these sentries fathers can name—
chrysanthemums and chicory, nasturtiums, lobelia—
all the beautiful bitter things
we were not made to taste or swallow.

Polar Vortex 2019

There's a primal kind of clarity
when the whole city closes down
and you survey from the driveway
your arctic neighborhood
a collage of distant latitudes

There's a heightened sensitivity
in wind chill 40 below
when the ghostly wisps
entwine your feet
when you feel them scratch your heels

when overhead this silent land
you overhear a high-pitched ring
like shearing through sheet metal skies

and high above this desert snow
you sense the arcing flight
of some albino creature
shrieking through the polar air

Just days ago
you disbelieved the augury of weather seers
their urgency to track this one
its swooping here and there

Now the sages pound the drums
deep within your blood-rushed ears
Keep vigilance out there
they warn Watch
you don't let it bite

MARY WILLIS

London, Ontario

If It Hadn't Been Summer

For weeks I had to keep walking
though I didn't feel led.
All the green pastures were open
and beside them the streams were open as well,
filled with their whitest flowers,
clouds too still and shining
to carry anything away

but we'd buried her on Canada Day
in the valley of the shadow
that shouldn't have recognized
a fifteen-year old yet

and I had to stay
in an enormous country space
where celebrations went on and on,
each day like a young girl
handing out lupines and dandelions,
free seasonal beauties I couldn't accept,
each night wiser, holding off
inside black satin sleeves
unruffled sprays of stars out of reach.

The whole world marked an occasion,
a spirit's preparation. Everywhere I turned
was the language of light, her favourite psalm,
the one I found I hadn't learned
right through, by Christ's heart too.

Water Lilies

They greet me by breath before sight,
warm fragrance preceding colour and form

like the Spirit moving elusively on dark water
until God said, *Let there be light*

and original light began a long transit through time,
its echo rippling endless ponds—
this commonplace one this morning—
drawing miracles vividly up
from mineral slime, rich pigments of mud
where night still douses roots
that have barely a dream of greening,
just an impression of quick radiance meant to be.

The sun tops the trees, a chill white disk—
its pre-recorded grace a dead giveaway?
I've seen too much to accept that
but I hang around waiting for something more definite today
than flat floating leaves,
a few buds, intact, glimmering

while I know even if waxy petals melt open,
disclose flaring joy at the heart
of transitory things, I'll want it to stay,

I'll feel illusory as Monet must have felt,
prey to persistent impressions, an old man

haunting his own gardens at Giverny,
peering through a glass darkly, age-thickened cataracts:
were the pigments always that grainy?
where is the deep taproot of fluent light?

Sometimes he must have stood on the edge of it all
like one of the votive cattails
ringing this pond without perfume or beauty,
offering himself, a paintbrush only
yet reassured that was enough,
soaking illumination in through every pore of his spirit,
so weighted in glory he didn't need to lift his arm
to stroke blue silky margins of the drifting sky.

Water Stories

It was often a dry land
that forgot its history of rain.
Men spoke with dust in their mouths
and women carried pitchers
on—or in—their heads,
dreamed of turquoise water

but Rebekah didn't dream of water walking
so far, finding her.
She didn't expect gold shimmers,
waves braceleting her wrists

and the Samaritan woman probably hoped
at most for a prophet someday
leading her to a river.
She didn't dare to ask
a river to change its course for her.
She never imagined it coolly resting on
her sunstruck neighbourhood well,
drawing its deepest prophecies
out through her.

Asymptote

At some point it comes to
just you and us.
We're walking our road to Emmaus
that despite false starts and backtracking
is linear, moves reasonably through time.

We believe we've left you
where you failed us, glory spent,
dead to our enterprise,
and even if subsequent reports are true
and you are alive, you must have moved beyond
the nail-studded lilies of Gethsemane
to heaven's luxuriant trees of life
safely pruned
by saints' transparent hands.

But then, with feet as dusty as ours,
you approach in disguise,
deliberately veiling our eyes,
curving in so close
you wholly occupy our blind spot
with your infinity of dark.

You force us to reopen the case,
read the evidence according to your point of view—
the one on trial, we think

until you start to walk on, apart
and we see the dependable night of earth
returning to lock us in.

It's our choice if the miracle will occur,
our line and your circle intersect.
We can hand you the key straight away,
you can turn time back,
the morning star can enter
our small stone house.

Great Blue Heron Standing

apparently disengaged in pond or rippled dawn,
one-legged like a tranced tree

yet power poised is dangerous.
This philosopher could turn blue-blooded archangel,
suddenly rise, throw the world off
for sheer brilliance of formless space

or instead dip inward
past the beaten-gold icon
to break the code of life,
fish out a shimmering piece
of the action, a breathing clue,
and swallow it whole.

Night Echoes

An owl seeks refuge
somewhere in the woods from light,
pulls darkness like a monk's cowl
over its head.
Only its voice issues,
spare, longing—

able to carry me anywhere,
places God doesn't want me to go?

I don't know
even that much
or if this is one of those times
a poem hoods itself as prayer
in the inarticulate night world
the two often share.

Her Rock Garden

She left it here
at the far end of the thin-grassed yard
like a spangled scarf dropped
on a hot August day.

I can't find the flowers,
though stones flecked with gold like lilies
mark their place.

I wish I could recall her design,
replant exact flashes of inspiration
along these blurred paths,

but I do remember the inherited text
of land my mother shared,
with overshadowing woods and clouded glory,
was more than a chapter
of marginal history.
It meant something closer to covenant.

Walking to the Beach

Kihei, Maui

You have to move slowly
as if you were already
wading into water,
into a tall blue shock,
the wave of a bright idea.

Under the plumerias
you pause, drenched,
lapped by the scents of dawn,
forgotten pools where you once
dipped your face and drank.

Shower trees attending you next
aren't there to confuse
with splashes of new hues,
but to wake you to creation's way
of catching quick breaths—

and morning glories dappling lava rocks
draw you deeper
beyond yourself.

Already you've swum so far,
afraid you'll never get back,

and yet you haven't even entered
into glory.

That's when Ezekiel's angel stops you,
returns you to the shore of the world
where everything is planted firmly
and nothing ever stops growing.

At day's end, still you will see
the sturdy stamen of the sky glowing

and later the pollen of stars.

Mace's Bay Revisited

Stunted trees still stand,
backs hunched to the Atlantic, to the wind
that single-minded as any wraith
is always pointing them inward.

Who's there? I'm tempted to ask,
looking for the exact place
the family used to picnic,
sheltered by rocky outcrops.

Unexpectedly, Jeremiah joins in:
Break up your fallow ground.
But this is stony—impossible—land!
He replies, *It is time to seek the Lord.*

Who could argue?

You and I sit side by side,
talk over lost time
and those missing to us
who have found God permanently.

Predictably, before very long
the sea gives up its mercurial sparkle,
the ghost of sun,
and Fundy's perennial border plant materializes,
succulent fog overhangs the shoreline.

We wind our way to the headland
where cranberries used to mist the ground.
My skin grows damp—
which makes me remember Jeremiah's promised reward
for those who seek the Lord:
a rain of righteousness.

Rain—not fog that hangs back from change.
I'm not sure I could forecast a shower
as clear and discrete as holiness

but the barometric pressure is perceptibly falling
and rain often starts as a drizzle
in the hard here and now.

MIHO NONAKA

Wheaton, Illinois

American Dream

Before dusk, I reached the diner.
I couldn't speak. I pointed to the plate
of the only other customer, an old man.
"Pancakes with two eggs sunny-side up?"
asked the waitress in a dusty rose uniform.
She called me "darling" even though we met
for the first time. His fork punctured one
of the runny suns, its yellow pooling on the edge
of the plate. The day nearly gone, like a bucket
dropped inside a long dried-up well.
Outside, a steel cross towered over
the crossroad of two highways.
"Where're you from?" The man stank of urine
and trash. I still can't answer his question.
Fireflies began to flicker in the sundown town.
Endless cornfields all hushed and taut
as if angels had been holding back the winds
from the four corners of the earth, withholding harm.

33

Easter Cherries

Far from home, weeping cherries started blooming
for the first time outside the church:
this is their fifth Easter in Chicago.

Not breathtaking like those clouds after clouds
of blush petals along the Sumida River,
but darker, wispy flowers drooping downward.

Still, our pastor insists on a cherry viewing.
The youth spread a mat under the trees, and
instead of traditional mochi balls in three shades,

we snack on stale, craggy cookies—a donation
from Costco, one of their tax reduction tools.
The pastor wants a picture with his wife

and two daughters, both single and perfectly
bilingual. They take turns translating jokes
and sermons into English for the non-Japanese

like my husband. Their mother calls them her
"kingdom soldiers," who partake of every
discomfort required of their parents' mission,

their untranslatable lives. The weeping branches
are nothing but an obstacle for our children;
they feel no longing when flowers scatter,

consumed in gathering cheap plastic eggs
strewn over the grass. Triumphant, my son holds
his Peeps like tiny pyramids in glittering sugar.

He understands, but does not speak my
mother tongue. Chick by chick, he tears off
and swallows its neon marshmallow body

while I wonder why I ever allowed myself
to believe that one day, I would feel less
alone. The pastor in his leather jacket might well

pass for a middle-aged Yakuza, if he'd not
one afternoon, received God's calling
in bone-dry California, waiting for an oil change

on his beat-up Toyota. Our elder, Mr. Aoki,
who lost his engineering job in the city just
before retirement, lectures on how to make

salted-cherry cakes using a bread machine.
Mrs. Aoki pours green tea in everyone's
Styrofoam cup, apologizing for its bitterness,

urging us to take more American cookies.
No saké accompanies our Easter cherry-
viewing, but the pastor's face has turned pink,

and in silence, we take in how much his
hairline has receded over the last year
or two. We have no lyres to hang on the trees

but our hearts. What opens our hearts to these
blossoms is their momentary pause
marked by the clarity of their leave-taking.

Sitting upright on the mat, his eyes tracing
the petals, another elder, Mr. Suzuki, whispers:
"Will there be such flowers in heaven?"

Heartland

Again late August, again cicadas are singing their
Songs as I step into the field.

I didn't know, in America, too, their voices would
Consume the summer's end like harsh grains

Of mineral, coursing the air, coming to
A stop, and then rising again from all directions.

Rarely do I forget which country I am in, but
This is one of the moments: bare feet against

Grass, hair undone, golden edges and
Rustling leaves around me, blurring my sense

Of borders. I am who I was when words were just
Words—though foreign—no emotion or judgment

Yet attached to them. How lonely I was, unafraid,
Believing that one day, I'd learn to sing them all.

Another song starts from who knows which tree
High above; sky darkens. Cicadas raise their voices,

Empty whatever is left of their liquid dreams
Underground, their selves now the ghost of the shells

Hooked on the wrinkled barks, their wings hardened,
Their hearts stretched over their segmented bodies.

I want to say, *I hear you*. Let me enter your song.
Let me grow more and more instrument-like

As the sound showers and seeps into my skin,
Each throat drying, hollowing me to the core.

My *Moby-Dick*

Don't give up. Whales
sing and dream of becoming
pocket-sized. Ancients
said a single whale
feeds a whole village.
Nothing wasted once
beached. You, wrecked
Noah's Ark of animal
flesh, you, giant
catfish under every
earthquake, God in details.
Headed to East or West?
Gashes along your body,
my body, host to colliding
squid beaks. Skinned,
gutted, your organs, my blubbers
on sale from our bloody house.
Professor, there is something
kabuki about Ishmael's voice
in the Japanese translation.
We are a vulgar art,
wartime fishy margarine,
the unborn whale in baby
kimono. A packet
of ritual salt blooms
at night: the ocean in a glass.
We dream of belonging
in all our impurities.

Water and Fire

No confusion, not drunk, never
fear when you feel
the water bubbling

from within. Each soul
is a well, set apart, alone.
The sun is directly over

head, and a stranger
waits for you at the well,
thirsty. He has nothing to draw

with, and the well is deep.
So is every other well,
he reminds you. It's not up to you

to decide whether you've
suffered long enough.
He knows your name,

doesn't he? Love comes
in tongues of fire. Flames
won't set you ablaze;

you will be unconsumed.
A pair of wings brush past
your eyes in silver flickers

as the sound of water nears.
Open your thirsty mouth.
He is offering your very self

in a glass, the same water that
connects every well flowing
between Father and Son.

The rushing water reverses
something of Babel
in each of us: an upturned

hourglass measuring
the immeasurable, holding
our shattered lives together.

The Night I Received Your Wedding Invitation

I smelled pollen in the air for the first time.
You once said you wanted to become
a lighthouse keeper and I said I would too.

Neither of us realized then, we couldn't live
near each other; people wouldn't need both lights
together. Dear friend, often I feel like

climbing the winding stairs alone
while the warm breath of flora
continues traversing mysteriously

between spaces. At twenty-seven,
I still haven't fathomed fruitfulness; perhaps
it comes gradually, like gentians followed

by golden motes, a foreign smell.
Who could your fiancé be? I pause under
the pine branches—so many soft needles about

to release their secrets. Almost a voice, the aimless
course of invisible specks. Tonight, the only thing
I can see are your pollen-dusted fingers.

Legion

I sleep-talk. I scare my family in the dark.
All sweetness gone, my voice deepens,
thick with ire. College friends would call me
Heidi who longs for the Alps, her gramps, stinky
goat cheese, sleepwalking like a ghost
in pajamas, far from home. But I sleep-
speak. I have voices I wish I hadn't. Once
Father told me I wailed in the voice of a samurai
drowning or being drawn out. I remember
nothing, just the fear, the pressure that binds me
in iced barbwire, turning into rage
like a sword I must have swallowed whole.
All I am keeps mouthing "Get out!"
in the tongues I know I don't know.

JEN STEWART FUESTON

Longmont, Colorado

Monologue of the Juno Probe

They have named me for a woman
who could pull the curtains back and peer
at the ineffable by inches.
I have one eye and broad wings for catching sun
and instructions to approach the god
slantwise to his poles.
Truth is come to by peregrinations
then a scurry to safety, flame faced and bright,
like Moses on the mountain glimpsing backside
of the Holy, like the woman grasping Jesus' robe
and slipping through the crowd
possessed of power and changed.
Perijove by perijove I dive into the clouds
and show you how they eddy,
how Jupiter's a turbulence of fire, how
we learn to circle toward a power
we cannot not describe or tether,
an orbit around what governs us
but we cannot touch. If we're careful
we can glimpse it
looking backwards as we go.

Trying to Conceive

Last month the test was negative and another you did not cohere.
They measured blood in little vials, gave me pills to make
the bleeding come or go and every day, I dipped a
sticky slip of paper in a little cup. They laid me
out on tables, peering in to see if you were
there. But you were not. There was not
even a you to not be, so nothing
has been lost at all. Just time.

It's hard to conceive how things might be
if you were. My belly growing taut and thick,
my mind arranging space for you in ordered lives,
and how we'd decorate, dust off the bassinette. But every
month's an otherwise, each possible eludes us, swept off like
seedlings washed downhill by rain. This, the nature of things. What
finally comes to being comes with shadows, carries with it all the absences
that rest in everything.

Nursling

After Psalm 131

When did I ever thirst as much?
Bend my body, thrash unwieldy
legs, wheel my arms to rock
toward a yielding warmth,
toward skin and gathering and milk?

Did I tune my ears to silence
when the singing stopped? My
newborn eyes still colorless
and dim, hungry for returning light.

No. I remember crying in the dark,
wandering empty hallways toward
my mother's room, trying
every door, my body weaned
off starlight now for good.

Postcard, Yellowstone

Corner of eye catches
the plume of smoke,
the pillar of steam
etched against Wyoming,
orange scratches down a painted sky.

I think about how
this rhythmical release
was caught by family photos:
my aunt in her patent leather shoes,
tilting head out over mud pots
boiling with sulfur.
Grandpa's thin, one-pocket shirts
tucked into khakis, arm cranking
the camera wheel. Images
flickering now in our collective memories

that we are people who go out to witness

who hold our breath and poise ready
to capture that instant
Old Faithful blossoms from the ground
where the pillar of
steam and fire paint the sky
again.

Walburga Catechism

The wind breathes hot on tumbles of red stone.
Dust exhales behind the combing plow, hay parts
in crescent rows. Paint on cross-beams peels
and cactus flowers wither in the wheat.

> *Why would the Word take on such heat-flushed flesh?*
> *So thus we might know love.*

I bend to pick up chunks of granite stone
and place them on each Station's cracking limb,
where moths cocoon in figures of reliefs,
white floss wraps linen shrouds across the beams.

> *How is it that the Son of God is man?*
> *St. Teresa said, Christ has no body but your own.*

So whose feet press this ground, and smooth the scorched
moss on the sun-turned bellies of the rocks?
Grasshoppers green at ankles, watching sisters
in their habits the same color as this sky.

> *How in wilderness can we speak the names of God?*
> *We can name God only by taking creatures as our starting point.*

So something unknown names itself in wind
that prays through windows of the church, the space
between the panes an open throat voicing
mercy in a high-pitched tongue, and I think
how misery and mercy sound the same.

> *Why did the Word take on flesh?*
> *Christ's body was finite, therefore the human face of Christ*
> *can be portrayed.*

When I was young, I remember hearing
of the crucifix, We should not glory
in his death, He's no longer on that cross.
No, I think, but we are. I want to smooth
his broken body in my hands and mouth
the sound of mercy like a round stone.

This place, this native ground of weeping, this
stretched blue and this bristled sage unhallowed
by history or name, but still angels
pass between red-tumbles of the boulders,
as new and bright arrivals to this air.

This is the only place where I can learn
to love, the only body given me
to wear. I carry it by habit through
this sky and try on every color's name.
Caught up in love of things invisible,
known only by resemblance to what's seen.

Detail of a Peacock

Nestling in the niche between the chapel's crumbling
arches, his long blue neck plucks nibbles of tessera.

He wanders through mosaic parables like something risen
out of time, wearing fashion all wrong for Byzantium—

a jaunty tri-plume hat in an age of halos. You presume
at first this must have been a gold-leaf sermon contra

vanity, or like those tapestry-arrested unicorns, an
attempt to tame our lusts of flesh. His sumptuous blue

feathers with their knowing eyes seem destined
for a harem girl's accessory, so what are they doing here?

What Augustine wrote at Carthage, though, unveils
the peacock's changing reputation, that before

its current turn as vain pretender, or the empty suit,
the Church discovered peacock flesh does not decay.

So poke at any early Christian tomb and there
they preen, depictions of life that does not die, the

incorruption of brief bodies made eternal. How every
year a feather's molt returns brighter and more beautiful.

This long-necked fellow settles into tessellation,
his plumage not quite all unfurled

so not to draw too much attention, but whispers that
he's hiding here for now, a creature caught

in colored bits of glass, waiting till these ruins
are restored to make his move.

To a Friend Lonely in the Fall

In fall at least the world doesn't lie to you
about dying, might even convince you you can
do it beautifully, become the blaze maple
transcendent against blue. The stands

of cottonwood that in summer appeared to be one
tree, unclasp green hands, separate and shiver
bare, remember they're alone. The light that angles
through the gold is not the kind that fills

the wanting in your core. Still, it can be caught
with words arranged on lines, like bait on hooks,
and fed upon. Because love is not a fullness, it's an
ache. Because one God I've known has loved me most

when He took everything away. The stark tree stripped
knows every name the wind goes by.

Dualism for Beginners

We don't choose what we believe in. Toddlers sing-song
you can't see me, you can't see me, even though
they've only closed their eyes. You know the soul
by how it wakes inside you when you're looking

in a mirror and you see yourself see you. This strange
unrecognition felt before you learn the difference
between mind and brain, that science can't locate
the part of us that knows its knowing. There must be days

this first makes sense, but children feel out such riddles
with their hands. Right there in chapter one, this earth
we think we're other than takes form, and we're an urge
of breath blown through the dust. The way a child plucks

dandelions and blows the star-shaped seeds through air.
They don't know they're made of earth until they fall.

JAMES TUGHAN

Oakville, Ontario

Snagged

> *For Glenn*

Bait cast, arcing softly
into the reeds and
into shallows full of life:
volumes of possibilities, suspended
beneath landing pads
between two worlds where
      dragonflies watch.

We wait for that:
that lunging swallow
of fresh ideas submerged, deeper
in shafts of light
in the pulsating current as
      fingerlings hide.

Knowing the rules
that life can be swift
in the inviting of death, poisoned,
we wish for pain where
the only familiar is that
      predators wait.

Incendiary

When you try to explain
the place that you come from:
where the children, the helpless
become wolves and defenders,
you meet only hunters, now
caught in headlights.

It seems so unreal
the place that you come from
to be guarding the parents
who've become children and users
asleep under quilting—not
seen after sunrise.

You accept the reversal
in this strange land you come from.
There are whole families of secrets
in the addicted and broken
in the tinting of glasses and
rheostat cooling.

Into this darkness —
slips, shoehorned as juggler
of lights and of visions with new
markers to freedom, to runways
of hoping—the Spirit ignites
fresh fire in the ice.

Pieta

For Donna

The angel said it, I put it away.
I could not know. How could I?
How does one raise a child
in a spirit of hopelessness?
How can one consider and accept
the unimaginable?

My people dream, they speak only of blessing:
of wise bounty from God's hand.
They see fertile fields of gleeful children
fruitful quivers in the young,
vines and bows fully laden.
They do not contemplate
the unimaginable.

Now here, my son lies silent
and scarred by a torrent of raging.
The angel said it. I put it away.
I buried that sword in a mother's dreams.
It will take time to comprehend, to fathom
the unimaginable.

Fly

For Alex

When I consider the few things
whose loss would leave me
so much less willing to live,
chief among them is the privilege
of watching you move:
effortlessly weaving through the traffic
of lesser minds laying claim
to this football.

I struggle still to describe
this grace, this reverence
you show for the room for breathing
that this object commands.
You seem to know its will
and all the places where its servants
are supposed to arrive
when directed there.

Your touch squares and sends it
almost without looking
fully expecting your mates
to see as you see, to know its path
its intended destination behind
a defender caught unawares:
one flick beyond
their dull imagining.

Mortar

For Sanballat

I will take the word of Jeremiah any day:
the great prophet who expended his manhood
and bled his heart dry, presiding over the death
of the proud and of the innocents,
slaughtered and burned with ruthless abandon
within the great city of God
within the walls of Jerusalem.

You thought you had lived to see the day
when the God of David was proven
to have gone completely AWOL.
You thought your incense-stained Molech
might actually have brought about the fall
of the great city of God, caving in
the great walls of Jerusalem.

You rejoiced with Nebuchadnezzar.
You watched them throw priests aflame
and screaming children too from the temple walls
into the crumbling rubble below.
You couldn't believe your good fortune
to see Solomon burning in the city of God
behind the walls of Jerusalem.

Now there is this upstart, cupbearer to Cyrus
raising the great stones again into place.
Nehemiah is on the winches now and you
oh Sanballat, cannot see or hear our God,
the God of angel armies circling all about
around the great City of God, raising again
the mighty walls of Jerusalem.

Fragile

For Rachel

All the way to Peterborough
the soft rain obscures what lies ahead.
The road gleams and dissolves
into the liquified brush strokes
of Monet's near blindness.

The rear warning lights
are a field of red poppies
dancing: they are mere impressions
of the vehicle I am following
from behind a curtain of tears.

Each wiper stroke erases the memory
of every delayed reaction, course correction,
or imagination of threat
awaiting your fragile condition:
 weaving past the double yellow line.

Welcoming Party

For Mark

The crowds—and even the sand flies—are deafening.
But you can't fool me. I can see you guys
at the back of the crowd, all decked out
in your finely groomed scowls
looking for all the world like orbiting wolves
waiting for an opening
to pick off a straggler.

Do you really think my head is spinning:
euphoric on Red Bull prophecy,
looking for an imminent throne,
courtiers and all the palace intrigues
that come with an inner circle?
But you go on imagining that I am here
competing in a forum of your design.

You really don't know
who you're dealing with: who it is
who rides on the backs of the prophets,
who it is who really holds the cards that
you think you're dealing.
I mind the store. I raise the lambs.
I hold the knife. I lay it down.

Abundance

For a donor

You once asked me outright:
clear and plain as the scent of your
breath, Gilbey's and Jabez flowing.
"Do you believe, do you believe
in abundance?"

I tread carefully, one foot on the brake,
and one foot in the door, fearful:
word and meaning carefully measured,
Have you forgotten, really forgotten the
distance? is what I am thinking.

In your bunker the concrete is still drying.
The gun port slit between us frames me
between naked exposure to the elements
and your comfortable shelter
of due diligence.

I am caught in open fields of fire.
I am alone like David, alone with the smell
of Saul, doing my time in the Negev,
alone but for the words of Samuel
ringing in my ears.

BILL STADICK

Watertown, Wisconsin

Almost Taking Eucharist

(At the funeral mass of a friend's mother)

First off, I am protestant.
I protest everything: sanctuaries that echo,
robes that billow, mothers who die —
especially mothers who die.

Second, I am Scottish. That bagpiping
of *Amazing Grace* in my left ear conjures
in my soul a heath-buried ancestor
who grins, using my lips.

Third, I once shared an office with her firstborn,
making headlines and junk mail. We listened to the loud
of Violent Femmes and Jethro Tull:
You can excommunicate me
on my way to Sunday school.

Because of this or despite this, I almost walk
the ten yards to the man in the dress. And I almost
register an official protest with the painted Jesus
hunched in the concavity that joins wall and ceiling.

Hunched as I hunch in the varnished pew,
Trying to mumble any of ninety-five theses.

Church / Body / Art

Due to sanctuary distances or my own weak eyes,
I can't quite make out which psalm one congregant
references on her left shoulder, but I have spent

entire sermons making ekphrasis of another's left triceps
and the wholly secular icon he let someone ink thereon:
a freakish skull with single shock of hair fountaining

from the crown. As I stare into the incarnadined eye
sockets of this *momento mori* acquired, no doubt,
on a much-earlier, devil-may-care evening of his finitude,

I scheme like a second-rate Sadducee my own trick
question for Jesus of Nazareth: *At the resurrection, will*
the glorified bodies of these two still sport their tattoos

as your glorified wrists still bear the nail prints? I believe
it would be a glorious thing. I think mnemonics would do us
all good. Even David, who has since no doubt written others

might enjoy seeing which from the original psalter she chose.
And even a glimpse of that biker bar skull on the other side
would send us into Sawdust Trail ecstasies every time.

Here again,
in this great hall,

in the kingdom
of this world,

here to hear,
most of all,

this advent's
recitation

of that two-
quarter rest,

(nothing more),
that shuddering

caesura, that
pause expect-

ant as the virgin
herself, which

heralds the final
four syllables in

*The Hallelujah
Chorus*, saying

the unsayable,
emboldening

us *not* to sing
along if we

know the

        silence.

How I Saturday in the Suburbs

I am taking part in a great experiment—whether writers can live peacefully in the suburbs and not be bored to death.

—Louis Simpson

From my deck, I work today's impossibly blue sky
as a sports analyst might work his monitor by finger-
circling any spot through which—bam—Christ might

return as promised or the double moves Michael et al
might make to thwart demonic advances. Yes, in fact,
this *is* how I Saturday while Neighbor A and his circular saw

whine-screech a shed into existence and Neighbor B push-
mows around an offspring who's springing, up and down,
up and down, up and down, on a rapture-ready trampoline.

and when again it doesn't end, the world, I head inside,
ignite the TV and sitcom away another day, wondering if
tomorrow the sky will get less boring, more biblical.

Ballad of the Church Potluck

Not that we think Fortune exists,
Nor would we e'er endorse
That evil weed they've nicknamed *pot*
For main or dessert course.

It's just a term to say we'll meet
With Tupperware and spoons
To put the devil in his place
On Lord's-Day afternoons

With casserole that's preordained
To dwell beside lime Jell-O
And silver silos of decaf
That's almost never mellow.

All to the praise of Jesus Christ
We'll eat and trade clean jokes
Under the aegis of a faith
We *know* can't be a hoax.

If Cephas came and brought Jan Hus,
They'd find two folding chairs
And marvel at that green dessert's
Pale, syrup-soakéd pears

And see in lieu of martyr-blood
These bowls of cherry punch,
Amazed that sacred history
Might lead to such a lunch.

My Father Went to New Jerusalem and All I Got Was This Lousy Poem

Now that he's in Kingdom Come, will he check out the Throne Room?
    I hear it's three parts incredible and one part fab.

Now that he's in Eternity, will he shop the Avenue of Many Mansions?
    I hear it's worth the myocardial infarction all by itself.

Now that he's in Glory, will he hire a guide to take him beyond the Great Beyond?
    I hear it's how one finds the rowdiest (no more) blues bars.

Now that he's in Heaven, will he get permission to post his grandchildren
just one card,
    as he did last fall from Oberammergau?

Arrival of the *Ville du Havre*

A shimmer first in the distance so inconsequential it might
be mistaken for the slow flapping of a tern above lazy waves.
Eventually, though, it becomes, even to weak eyes, a steamship
bulking larger and ever more defined until one can make out crew
and passengers on deck, can hear the patient crescendo of voices
blending into that gospel song so many had loved so profoundly
during the flawed years of their scarred lives. Even before one sees
the name stenciled on its side, we know this vessel's backstory,
what had transpired at 47°21′ N 35°31′ W on 22 November 1873,
have heard the haunting narrative of the drowned Spafford girls—
Annie, Maggie, Bessie and Tanetta—retold in reverential cadences
by ministers of music without number. Yet, here comes *that* ship,
almost to haven now, almost out of the sorrows of that sea,
those on shore now close enough to take the echo of the refrain:

Ship: *It is well.*

Shore: *It is well.*

Ship: *With my soul.*

Shore: *With my soul.*

Then, in quavering unison: *It is well, it is well, with my soul.*
In the ensuing bustle of disembarkation, streamers litter the scene,
fluttering, flickering and settling on the waters, dock-planks
and shoulders of one Attending Angel who, grinning, brushes
them off as necessary debris from the most mind-blowing gig
he's worked since that whole *this same Jesus* thing on Olivet,
who's now escorting the four girls through the hooting hoopla
to a family reunion set to anthemic music that would all be
too Hollywood an ending were it Hollywood

or ending.

The Sin–Boldly–Bulwark–Never–Failing Blues

I just   opened the can of worms that will eat my flesh

I just   shrugged *it's all good* and my nose started Pinnochioing

I just   passed my annual physical and failed my annual spiritual

I just   peeked into my closet and one of its skeletons whispered
        It's me, Uriah

I just   vomited after winning a humble pie eating contest

I just   tried talking my way out of eternal damnation as I would
        a parking ticket

I just   called to say I'm sorry (I got caught)

I just   justified shouting *raca* at my neighbor because his fallen leaves trans-
        gressed boundaries

I just   can't stop myself from saying *I just*

I just   confronted all my demons and they doggedly refused to settle out of
        court

I just   plugged in another household god that's blaring *mea culpa non. mea
        maxima culpa non*

I just   remembered 1521

I just   reread Habakkuk 2:4

I just   ordered me a heaping helping of alien righteousness

I just   keep repeating *hier stehe, ich kann nicht anders* and *yum*

Hauntingly Misshapen Poem

> *(On learning my ancestor was hanged as a witch
> in Dorchester, Massachusetts in 1650)*

this is
not easter
wings at
least not
yet this
is what is
penned
when you
find they
broke

your
mother's
father's
mother's
mother's
father's
father's
father's
father's
father's
father's
mother's
neck
and all
you can
do now
is break
some
lines
to ask
how did
this fall
further
any flight
in her

BURL HORNIACHEK

Selkirk, Manitoba

Living in a Secular Country

> *The only physical theories we accept are the beautiful ones.*

—Albert Einstein

We live in a darkened world, an age when God's
Discernable presence, like the slow but powerful bear,
Seems safely deposed to its arctic den.
Modern thought breeds materialism,
That dull song played on winter's harp,

But clues to a coming spring abide:
None can answer how the mind's small flower
Greens itself out from matter's frozen turf,
Nor how beauty's arrow flies, almost
Without fail, straight to the eye of truth.

I know that here, in this frozen land,
Eternal June shall play again its lusty theme.

Eve

The mother of us all
Also gave birth to the fall,
For the giver of life
Is also the giver of pain and strife.
We step toward the grave with every breath;
The blessing of life cradles the curse of death.

Fire Down on the Labrador

After Newfoundland artist David Blackwood's etching

The sea is enchanted.
Its water is luminous, if cold.
Every fleck is veiled
In a whisper of twilight,
Saying, "This is a place lost
To you as myth or legend."

Here the ice drifts on,
Asleep in its watery bed,
A ballet of light
Upon crystal boulders.

The fire on the ship burns,
Ferocious, but insignificant.
Only a whale,
Snug in his apartment
Of blubber,
Dares wager a smile amid all this cold.

What country is this?
Were they men such as us
Who ventured like pallid ghosts
Onto these liquid pastures,
Who tossed themselves
Like dice onto the sea?

They were. And if we have not
Like them set sail
On these dark, abysmal plains,
Let us go into the world as they went still:
Full of spirit, full of hope,
Venturing with gladness
Into the lonely, inhospitable places of earth.

Norval Morrisseau

Here are brushes that speak
The grammar of earth,
Lines that laugh themselves
Into birds or beasts,
All of the natural world
Dipped in the medicine of colour.
We see men swim in the souls of beasts,
Night sleeping in the souls of men,
Stones preaching to us in pigment,
Flowers that are whispered explosions of light.

What vision took you to this place?
What spirit guided you to the lodges of dream,
Spoke to you these things?

"Your eye will become voice.
Beaver, thunderbird, bear and trout,
All will speak through your lines.
The murmurings of tree and stream
Will nestle deep in your canvas.

Carry their thoughts into the world of men."

To John Keats

The myth-bird, slaying my soul with its chant,
Filling the waste of night with an ache eager
To bliss the world with its soothing grief.
Keats, you knew such evenings too.

Hard is the school of melancholy, this anvil
On which our souls are wrenched, beaten, and shaped
Into their proper selves. Yet, you survived, and more,
Putting the knife of verse to these dark materials,
Paring them down to an essential art.
Rejoice! One must be a diver of great strength
To have fished such pearls from an ocean of grief.

Gethsemane

As, in dark earth, Eden wombed the first man,
So shall this hour of agony and triumph bear,
Into new light, a new son, greater than his prime.

As new seed spoiled the limit of Eve's core
So shall a newer promise break from earth's shade,
The garden labouring its fruit to air.

As a bride who has waited long for her groom
So has suffering groped to this banquet hour,
The seed of hope planted in her ghastly soil.

Caravaggio

Yours was a world filled with death,
Where every alley throbbed with danger,
And every church was packed with sinners.
You were there,
A quarrelsome man
Making your way among popes and plagues.

You took it all in,
Dining with burglar and bishop,
Painting for God while living in the gutter.

We can see what you loved:
Ripe bodies and rotten fruit,
Flesh that glowed like a candle,
The whole world decaying into beauty.

This is the world as it is,
Filled with stupidity and sin,
But awake with feeling,

And almost redeemed by your being alive.

Rodney Bay Marina, May 21, 2012

For Carlos Fuentes

Night spills its ink upon the sky.
My friends, it is you and I
Who sit by the sea's warm,
Soft, and tranquil body. There is no storm
Tonight as we sit by the bay,
And chatter about the events of the day.

There is no need.
We carry such weather within us: life, age, despair,
Thoughts of lovers who are not here,
And of Carlos, who came here to talk and to drink,
Like we, and now does sink
Silent beneath the meed.

We turn away and laugh.
The glassy lights still glare
From all the boats at anchor there.
Dark thoughts are tossed away like chaff.

But his fate is ours; it *must* be.
Old and young,
These makers of beauty will soon be gone
Like a spangle of sun
Darting across the Caribbean Sea.

The Point of Words

The point of words is that they stretch
A bridge from soul to soul,
As rivers of purest silence slice
The part from off the whole.

When words just stumble sound to sound,
The bridge will barely hold.
The other shore is far away;
The waters deep and cold.

Vicious Geometry (Picasso)

You wielded style like a scalpel,
Gave us reality dismembered,
Womankind sliced into cubes,
Their faces like monkeys,
Or pressed into the mold
Of a vicious geometry:
Beauty offended you.

Then war gave you its perfection,
Guernica, where we see typed up
The full abstract of an annihilation:
Beasts nothing but bloody chunks,
And men nothing but shards of pain.
Suffering here returns as a god.

But I see more:
Sketches with the serenity of a Greek god,
Sunshine splashing on milk-white skin,
Bright guitars beside delicate girls,
Soft words and sweeter songs,
Tenderness even among desecration.

Joy is here, elusive, held at a distance,
But always dancing between the lines.

Crap

First of all, it exists, which, though in
Lower degree, is some kind of good,
For even the merest scent of worth
Speaks some ultimate as its final measure.

Even its genius for disintegration
Mirrors the infinite, a rich instability
Thrilled with potential to nutrient grass,
Tree, fruit, vegetable and luscious plant,
Nimble zeal infused into living form.

Being and change alphabet what is beyond them both:
The meanest lump of turd shelters enough
Goodness to prove the existence of God.

A Divine Poem

Bring down the fierce pressure of divine love.
As the heavy earth knits coal into diamond,
The immense weight bearing down, focused
To a single point where crystal leaps from dust,
So let your love remake my soul, the vice
Of your compassion press ash to gem.
As iron is torn from the ore, the grasping
Fingers of heat rescuing sweet metal
From its deep and chemical coffin,
So let my soul be smelted, blasted, burned
And all its pure and radiant elements of good
Be wrested away from their compounds of sin.
Let not one speck of my soul escape, but tear,
Break, raze, rake, pound, smash, burn. Upend all things.
Let not one stone remain in its place. Show
All must be broken to be bound up again.

SUSAN COWGER

Cheney, Washington

A Curious Win

From what strange land did fire emerge
In the beginning   no one says a word

About light gone mad   somewhere inside
An inferno bellows

The blast of singe brimstones heaven to one side
While the world cowers and waits it out

Tankers and hotshots take on faith
Reason empties a garden hose on the holocaust

Every war ends this way
Evergreens skeletal

Stripped of all save a few ragged cones
Held hostage by scorch

Dropping their seed
Fearlessly

Learning the Lord's Prayer

Come now your kingdom   please let it be
Montana or heaven   or something like that
An icy lake above timberline
Reflecting your face
        Is this what you're thinking
I'm thinking of the Pryor Mountains just there
Along the horizon to the south   elongated blue
A little bluer than sky   I'm seeing heaven on earth
Manageable at a distance   but immovable
The way prayer feels like a promise
Racing through prairie sage
The only place left where one can capture and keep
Wild horses   Daddy said do it
And it was ours
He didn't blink or snigger   though I imagine some mirth
In the power of yes
Yes   smack in the face of no way in hell
It was up to me   and it still feels that way
Like he wants it   hopes I'll give it a go

My Father Disappears

Canada geese circle the lake
And underscore the collapse of a sunset
Everything going down
A skirr of feathers   feet forward
Pinions flare   fold and tuck
For the imminent running-waddle

Geese on the ground don't look up
They swivel toward movement
Shadows and unexpected coyotes
Honking ensues   so like family
When death approaches
The flapping and noise signals

Giving up every bit of blue sky
A lifetime of savings
And something called home
No more than feathers
Slipping through the invisible

The Unknown Language

Sangre de Cristo   Cascades
Granite Peak to Sunlight Basin
The Bitterroots and Bighorns
Mountains I call my angels
Towers of pomp and majesty
Fawned over as if any one of them
Gives a rip   our imperial assumptions
Always one-sided   I call it
Church of the Missing Door
Where a piebald eaglet waits
For what has been killed to come to him
Seeds melted from resin's captivity
By fire   irresistibly grow and grow
I call yips back to the coyote   and name the black bear
Muggins   hoping for that kind of an in
A charm or goose bump to signify
I'm with them   and we   are *we*
From one and the same mind
This sort of reckoning is easy until you try
To get anything from the silence   like if it's true
No one's talking
While all that goodness echoes off the breastbone

Change the Color of Sky

It's black, but still Christmas at seventy-five
miles per hour, through Montana midnight,
the small drag of oh no pulls the long hope
of home off an icy December road in a spray of gravel,
a whirling wedge of light circling
the shriek no one heard, three thousand
pounds rasping rubber against sod, steel
crushed into clay, cheat grass and sage,
rocks, ground, then floating, flying free,
everything broken
against the power pole: foreheads and glass, ribs and time,
the brittle spine of the guitar packed against
a trunk of epiphany, honey and jam, the wooly new scarf
and baby Jesus, that chunky steel coffee mug
flung forty-five feet out the back window. It's waking,
upside down, voices and vertigo,
unable to breathe or unstrap from dust and
the dangle of sparks, and one, only one call
makes it through this black hole, someone shouting,
shouting my name, searching for us with headlights,
from the old road; errant oxygen bites through
a chest wall, silencing the howl of a lung's
collapse, how many times 1, 2, 3 lift, again lift;
the mercy of being almost there, a palm on the face
in lieu of morphine, an airlift
they call it while crooning soon, soon enough,
you're above the wreckage and weather,
watching the slow motion of earth, and
now, a gentle turn into the rising sun.

God as Water

Sometimes God is a pool
Where the cheeky swimmer dares to lie
On the surface   buoyant

And no one thinks a thing of it
When God rivers a careful wader deeper
No footings   no holds

But the kick-scream choke of an innocent falling in
Lungs conceding to rip-tide   broken teeth
And ragged questions bleed from the scrapes

Wounds ground into sand swell oh the swells
When God is ocean
Beauty and power that breaks

Every perfect shell
And shores its way into willful lungs until you know
God is flood

Infinite   unbound   weight over my head
And the unanswerable question

Thirst

Black Hills Dust

Gathering oomph he shuffles
To the roadside lookout   scans
The vast shimmer of emerald and blue
Sky facing up from the water
He shades his brow with a hand
Stares beyond sun-splattered waves
Ignoring verdant copses
Over basalt cliffs
Soldiering one end of the lake
Still solid   but silent
And squinting   the old man searches
Ancient accomplishments of creation
For a few molecules he left there
Something to gather in his hands
Wipe off with his hanky
And entrust to us for safe keeping after he's gone
We came here every summer he says
His last attempt
To hand over the best
Of earthly treasure

Happiness Carried on My Back

I hear your song so seldom
Sweet little call so softly dissolved
Roundest drop with a glistening fall

Plummet of waking alone in the night
Murmur of wind and wings
A curl of smoke and tenebrous calls

A slender thread swings in the dark
Clapper of glass and a silver bell
Lo a great presence stirs

Lifts its head   and nuzzles my neck
And lays its great crown back to slumber
Where just out of sight and never in front
I feel you breathing forever

January

Elbow on the kitchen table
She cradled the orb in her palm
She says to him   *I am nothing*

He watches her catch on the wound
Slide a thumb under the skin
And open the flesh

She strips the cover in one long peel
And curls the wrapper back
Into a semblance of wholeness

Slumped and squatty
She wrenches the pith apart
Separates her life into segments

Even the sweetest juice
Burns raw hangnails on her hands
She shoves the whole lot his direction

He arranges the fruit
Picking up each slice
Savoring   swallowing

They sit quietly touching hands
Listening to time
The fathomless globe between them

From the Rimrocks Over Billings

    Florid clouds

    Turn evening westward

A canon of vermillion flares

And burns magenta

Go ahead and say what you're thinking

    Oh God

    Is that you

Scorching the edge of everyone's page

In a scene so red

No one can look away

    Mirage

    Or miracle blooming

Through the dust and smoke   honestly

No one will turn to embrace the dimday behind them

It's okay if you weep

    For want of words

    There are no words here

It's really nothing   or the very last thing

The way we stare at gold

In reverence   waiting

    For something Almighty

    To speak

ABOUT THE POETS

Ryan Apple lives in Lansing, Michigan, where he is employed as a music professor at Great Lakes Christian College. An avid guitarist, his recording of works from the 1300s through the present day is available on iTunes and through his website. His poetry has been published or is forthcoming in a number of journals, including *Acorn, Time of Singing, Poems for Ephesians* and *Portage Magazine,* as well as in the Poemia Poetry anthology *Adam, Eve, and the Riders of the Apocalypse.* Read more at www.ryanapple.net.

Susan Cowger speaks the languages of both visual art and poetry. An abstract/impressionist artist, decades ago, Susan found verbal musings hung out well with ever-present visual questions. One seemed to lead to the other, gifting the viewer/reader with sometimes wonderous entry points. Word images eventually morphed into poetry. Art and writing eventually grew independent but parallel each other pondering Christian spiritual conundrums. Susan has commissioned paintings in both private and corporate collections. Her most recent writing appeared in *Ekphrasic Review, Windhover, Adanna, Perspectives, Crux*, and *McGuffin*. Susan is founder and past editor of *Rock & Sling: A Journal of Witness*. Her chapbook, *Scarab Hiding*, was released December 2006. Exchange thoughts? scowger@icloud.com.

Jen Stewart Fueston is a writer and teacher from northern Colorado. She teaches writing, rhetoric and literature—most recently at the University of Colorado, Boulder, and also previously abroad in Hungary, Turkey, and Lithuania. She publishes regularly in anthologies and journals such as *Ruminate, Christian Century*, and *Mom Egg Review*. She is a Pushcart Prize nominee, and published her first chapbook, *Visitations,* with Finishing Line Press in 2015. Her second, *Latch,* was published by River Glass Books in 2019. You can find more of her work at jenstewartfueston.com.

Laura Reece Hogan is the author of the poetry chapbook *O Garden-Dweller* (Finishing Line Press, 2017), and *I Live, No Longer* I (Wipf & Stock, 2017), which explores the spirituality of Paul the Apostle. Both books received 2018 Catholic Press Association awards. Laura's poems can be found in or are forthcoming in *America, The Christian Century, The Cresset, Saint Katherine Review, Anglican Theological Review, The Windhover, Poems for Ephesians, Penwood Review, PILGRIM: A Journal of Catholic Experience, Riddled with Arrows,* and other publications. Her poetry has been nominated for Best of the Net and a Pushcart Prize. Find her online at www.laurareecehogan.com.

Burl Horniachek was born in Saskatoon, Saskatchewan, and grew up in central Alberta. He has a degree in Ancient Near Eastern Studies from the University of Toronto, and studied creative writing with Derek Walcott at the University of Alberta. He has a strong interest in translation, especially Hebrew poetry from both the Biblical and Medieval periods. He has had poems and translations published in *Poetry East, Poetry International, Literary Imagination, TransLit, The Dark Mountain Project* and others. He lives in Selkirk, Manitoba. He may be contacted at: burlhorniachek@gmail.com.

Miho Nonaka is a bilingual poet from Tokyo. Her first book of Japanese poems, *Garasu no tsuki,* was a finalist for Japan's national poetry prize, and her poetry in English has been nominated for a Pushcart Prize. She is the author of *The Museum of Small Bones* (forthcoming: Ashland Poetry Series, 2019); her poems and essays have appeared in various journals and anthologies, including *Missouri Review, Southern Review, Kenyon Review, Ploughshares, American Letters & Commentary, Iowa Review, Tin House,* and *American Odysseys: Writings by New Americans* (Dalkey Archive Press, 2013). She is an associate professor of English and creative writing at Wheaton College.

Debbie Sawczak has been writing poetry since high school and is an admirer of Hopkins, Donne, and Kenyon. Her poems have appeared in such publications as *Crux, Writual, the U.C. Review,* and the *McMaster Journal of Theology and Ministry;* online at McMaster Divinity College's *Poems for Ephesians;* and in the anthology *Adam, Eve, & the Riders of the Apocalypse.* She has also enjoyed exposure through countless public readings, including the Eden Mills Writers' Festival, community events, coffee houses, and church liturgies. Debbie's work as a bookseller and professional editor gives her additional pathways into the beloved and stimulating world of text. A member of the Ecclestone writing group (Brampton, Ontario), she is married and has three adult sons.

Bill Stadick has published poetry, fiction and creative nonfiction in many publications, including *Barren Magazine, The Windhover, First Things, Christian Century, The Ekphrastic Review, Christianity and Literature* and *The Cresset*. His work has also appeared in the anthology, *Imago Dei: Poems from Christianity and Literature*. In addition, the poem, *The Sin-Boldly-Bulwark-Never-Failing Blues*, won second place in *Christian Century*'s 2017 Reformation Poetry Contest. He also has a chapbook soon to appear from Finishing Line Press. He founded and writes for Page 17, a marketing communications firm. Email: billstadick@gmail.com. Twitter: @bstad.

James Tughan is primarily known as a visual artist working in mapping of the northern Ontario wilderness with chalk pastels, as a cartographic realist. This work celebrates attachment to visible surfaces and the less visible human psyche, through a careful use of metaphor. He is an extensively published editorial illustrator (*Rolling Stone, GQ, House and Garden, Saturday Night, Financial Post Magazine,* and *Atlantic Monthly*) and an art educator and administrator, (Sheridan University, Redeemer University College Tyndale Seminary and College, and The Semaphore Fellowship). More recently, poetry has enabled him to articulate more directly certain aspects from his visual imagery of the world of persons, both in terms of overview and intimacy. He self-publishes under Nadir Press, in hand-made chapbook form available at tughanj@gmail.com.

Mary Willis spent her formative years in the beautiful Saint John River Valley of New Brunswick and the Green Mountains of Vermont. While doing degrees at the Universities of Vermont and New Brunswick, and at Brown University, she worked with the poets T. Alan Broughton, Fred Cogswell, Edwin Honig, and Keith Waldrop. She has published three chapbooks through Fiddlehead Poetry Books, including *Earth's Only Light*, and has recently written a novel, *Daughters in the Field*. Her poems have appeared in *Canadian Literature, The Fiddlehead, Pulp Literature* and other journals and have been anthologized in *Stubborn Strength* and *The Atlantic Anthology*. She lives in London, Ontario and may be contacted at: marywillisbooks@gmail.com.

ACKNOWLEDGEMENTS

I am grateful to Jill Peláez Baumgartner for her suggestions as I was finalizing my choices for this collection. The following poems previously appeared in these publications:

Ryan Apple

Orchards Poetry Journal—"Sonnet;"

Peninsula Poets—"Sundown;"

— "Portrait of a Friend's Daughter, Senior Year" was first prize winner of the 2018 Chaparral Poetry Contest, St. George, Utah.

— "Sundown" was reprinted in *Poems For Ephesians*.

Susan Cowger

Adanna Journal—"January;"

Crux—"Happiness Carried on my Back;"

The Windhover—"Learning the Lord's Prayer;"

— "The Unknown Language" appeared in the anthology *Surprised by Joy* (Wising Up Press, 2018).

— "Change the Color of Sky" appeared in Susan Cowger's chapbook *Scarab Hiding* (2006, Finishing Line Press).

Jen Stewart Fueston

Christian Century—"Dualism for Beginners," and "Monologue of the Juno Probe";

The Cresset—"Detail of a Peacock"

Rock & Sling—"Nursling";

Ruminate—"Postcard, Yellowstone," and "Trying to Conceive;"

Rust & Moth—"To a Friend, Lonely in the Fall;"

—"Detail of a Peacock" was reprinted in *Poems For Ephesians*;

—"Postcard, Yellowstone" also appeared in Jen Stewart Fuston's chapbook *Visitations* (2015, Finishing Line Press);

—"Trying to Conceive" and "Nursling" also appeared in Jen Stewart Fuston's chapbook *Latch* (2019, River Glass Books).

Laura Reece Hogan

Christian Century—"Organic Ink;"

The Cresset—"The Eyes I Have Desired;"

The Windhover—"Cherith," "Nocturne," and "Litany of Flights;"

—"Nocturne," and "Organic Ink" have also appeared in Laura Reece Hogan's chapbook *O Garden-Dweller* (2017, Finishing Line Press).

Burl Horniachek

Dark Mountain—"Norval Morrisseau"

Poetry East—"Caravaggio," and "Vicious Geometry (Picasso)."

Miho Nonaka

The Missouri Review—"Easter Cherries," and "Heartland;"

Tokyo Poetry Journal—"My Moby-Dick."